THE EVOLUTION OF FOOD

JEN BREACH

Before Reading: *Building Background Knowledge and Vocabulary*

Building background knowledge can help children process new information and build upon what they already know. Before reading a book, it is important to tap into what children already know about the topic. This will help them develop their vocabulary and increase their reading comprehension.

Questions and Activities to Build Background Knowledge:

1. Look at the front cover of the book and read the title. What do you think this book will be about?
2. What do you already know about this topic?
3. Take a book walk and skim the pages. Look at the table of contents, photographs, captions, and bold words. Did these text features give you any information or predictions about what you will read in this book?

Vocabulary: *Vocabulary Is Key to Reading Comprehension*

Use the following directions to prompt a conversation about each word:

- Read the vocabulary words.
- What comes to mind when you see each word?
- What do you think each word means?

Vocabulary Words:

- consuming
- convenience
- industrialized
- productive
- sustainable
- techniques

During Reading: *Reading for Meaning and Understanding*

To achieve deep comprehension of a book, children are encouraged to use close reading strategies. During reading, it is important to have children stop and make connections. These connections result in deeper analysis and understanding of a book.

 Close Reading a Text

During reading, have children stop and talk about the following:

- Any confusing parts
- Any unknown words
- Text-to-text, text-to-self, text-to-world connections
- The main idea in each chapter or heading

Encourage children to use context clues to determine the meaning of any unknown words. These strategies will help children learn to analyze the text more thoroughly as they read.

When you are finished reading this book, turn to the next-to-last page for **After-Reading Questions** and an **Activity**.

TABLE OF CONTENTS

FROM HANDMADE TO MASS PRODUCTION

Humans have been **consuming** animal milk for more than 6,000 years. For all that time, the products that are made with animal milk—milk, cream, butter, and cheese—have hardly changed. What has changed, though, is the process of milking.

consuming (kuhn-SOOM-ing): eating or drinking something

An average cow produces about 6.3 gallons of milk each day. That's about 350,000 glasses of milk in its lifetime!

Up until about the 1970s, animals had been milked by hand for thousands of years. It took an hour for one person to milk about six cows. Butter and cheese were handmade, too, and required a lot of manual work. Toward the end of the 20th century, robots were introduced to help speed up the milking process.

By the early 1990s, many cows, goats, and sheep in the United States were being milked by robots, called "automatic milking systems" (AMS). One AMS could milk one hundred cows in an hour. This change meant that dairies could increase their herds and reduce their work forces. Machines were soon used to separate cream, churn butter, and wash curds for cheese, too, making dairies even more **productive**.

productive (pruh–DUHK–tiv): making a lot of products, accomplishing a lot of work

FROM GREENGROCER TO SUPERMARKET

Hundreds of years ago, flour didn't come in bags and eggs didn't come in cartons. Shopkeepers would weigh out flour, oats, and sugar for customers right in the store. Customers would visit several stores to get everything they needed: a butcher for meat, a fishmonger for seafood, a greengrocer for fruit and vegetables, a bakery for bread, and a dry goods store for soap, sugar, and boxed goods. Milk, eggs, and cheese were delivered right to people's homes.

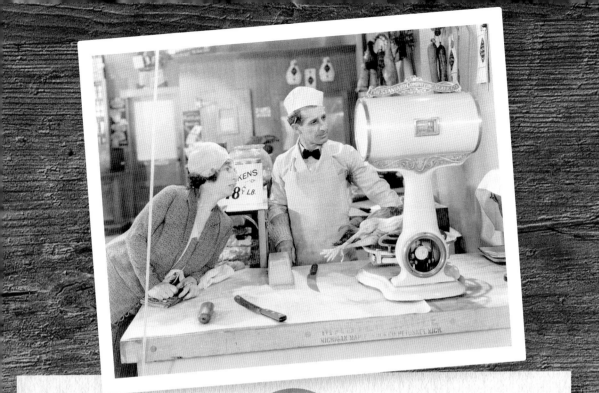

ROLLING DOWN THE AISLES

People used to carry all of their groceries in handheld baskets. But, with groceries becoming heavier and larger, a better solution was needed. In 1936, two men in Oklahoma got creative and came up with an idea. It was a basket on wheels. And just like that, the shopping cart was born!

In the mid-1910s, new self-service grocery stores offered prepackaged portions of flour, and customers picked out their own produce. Supermarkets, which combined all food shopping into one store, became common in the 1940s. Shoppers loved the **convenience**!

convenience (kuhn–VEEN–yuhns): something that makes a job or situation easier or more pleasant

MARKETING TO THE MASSES

Today's supermarkets are very carefully designed. Produce and flowers by the entrance make shoppers think of freshness. Products aimed at kids are strategically put on lower shelves at kids' eye level. Some companies pay extra to have their products placed in a highly visible area, like on the end of an aisle.

FROM SUSTAINABLE TO INDUSTRIAL . . . AND BACK AGAIN

Before the 1900s, farming practices in the United States hadn't changed much for over 10,000 years. But early in the 1900s, agriculture started becoming **industrialized**. Farmers began using synthetic fertilizers, chemical pesticides, crop specialization, and genetically modified seeds that would produce more food. Food became cheaper, but these practices were not good for the environment.

industrialized (in-DUHS-tree-uh-lized): the use of machines and factories; usually results in more profit but increased environmental harm

Around the middle of the century, raising animals also became industrialized. Free-range grazing was replaced by grain and corn-based feed. Animals were injected with antibiotics so they would grow faster and not get sick while living in cramped, dirty feedlots or on battery farms.

In recent years, **sustainable** farming practices and the use of organic products have made a comeback. Consumers concerned with their health and animal welfare are buying organic foods. Farmers concerned about the environment and global warming are using more environmentally friendly farming practices.

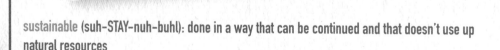

sustainable (suh-STAY-nuh-buhl): done in a way that can be continued and that doesn't use up natural resources

KNOCK, KNOCK! DELIVERY!

In 2020, the COVID-19 pandemic changed the way a lot of Americans got their food. With worldwide lockdowns and social distancing, home delivery of restaurant food skyrocketed, and food delivery companies were busy!

Grocery home delivery became very popular during the pandemic, too, both for grocery stores and online grocery services. While grocery stores employ workers to pick and pack orders, most online services use robots, which is cheaper.

Some consumers are skipping the grocery store altogether and buying their food directly from the farm. They buy a share of a Community Shared Agriculture (CSA) that gives them access to fresh food right from a local farm. Every week, a box of seasonal fruits and vegetables, meat, dairy, pasta, coffee, tea, and more is delivered to them or ready for pickup at the farm. It really doesn't get any fresher than this!

INNOVATION *AND* THE FUTURE

BEEP! BEEP! DELIVERY!

At dozens of college campuses around the country, students can have food delivered right to their dorm or study location by a rover-like robot! Students order using an app, and the robot uses maps, GPS, and motion sensors to safely navigate sidewalks, curbs, pedestrians, and crosswalks to deliver food right from the campus restaurant.

TV EATS

Nothing changed the role of food for American families more than TV.

In the mid-1950s, when 65 percent of American homes had a TV set and many women had entered the workforce, quick and easy TV dinners emerged. These were the first frozen dinners. They came on an individual foil tray with compartments for meat and gravy, vegetables, bread, and more. They were warmed in the oven and meant to be eaten in front of the TV.

Then, in the 1960s, food found a place *on* TV with cooking shows. Many of these shows featured famous international chefs who introduced people to new cooking **techniques** and cuisine from other countries.

By 1993, cooking shows, documentaries about food, and, of course, cooking competitions had become so popular that a brand-new network was launched— the Food Network. Anyone with a passion for food or cooking could be on TV.

techniques (tek-NEEKZ): methods or ways of doing something that require skill

INNOVATION
AND
THE FUTURE

BEHIND-THE-SCENES TASTING

Since one-hour cooking competition shows can take 12 or more hours to film, the final dishes that we watch the judges eat are usually cold. So even though they take a bite of the final dish, this isn't the first time they've tasted it. They have been tasting the contestants' food throughout the day while it's hot and fresh.

Cooking is very popular online too. Anyone from famous chefs to amateur kid chefs can post cooking videos on YouTube, TikTok, Twitch, and other online platforms. Whether you want to learn a new cooking technique or post your own cooking video for others to watch, it can be done on the internet.

INNOVATION AND THE FUTURE

— EAT LIKE A CARTOON —

Did you know that there are internet cooking videos of chefs recreating foods from some of your favorite TV shows? You can learn how to make Krabby Patties from *SpongeBob SquarePants*, Jake's Perfect Sandwich from *Adventure Time*, or Brock's Onigiri from *Pokémon*.

IMPOSSIBLY MEATY?

If you think it's impossible to make a hamburger without beef, or cheese without dairy, think again. Plant-based foods that mimic animal-based products like meat, milk, and cheese can be found in almost every grocery store. Often made with nuts, vegetables, and grains, plant-based products are a great choice for people trying to consume less meat and dairy. They're better for the environment too; each meatless patty gives off 12 times fewer greenhouse gas emissions, uses 50 times less water, and uses roughly 20 times less land than an animal product.

Food and food production have come a long way since hand milking and fishmongers. What changes will take place in the next 100 years?

Since cattle almost constantly give off gas—from both ends—they are responsible for almost 15% of all global greenhouse gas emissions.

HOW TO MAKE

HOMEMADE BUTTER

— INGREDIENTS —

4 cups heavy cream
1 teaspoon sea salt

— INSTRUCTIONS —

1. Fill a jar with a screw-top lid about halfway with the heavy cream. Secure the top. Now, shake the jar hard! Keep shaking until the cream starts to clump together into yellow chunks (butter). You'll see white buttermilk that has separated.

    You can also do this step using a hand beater, or in a food processor with a blade. To do this, add the cream and process on high until the buttermilk separates from the butter (about 5 minutes for the food processor, longer for the hand mixer or jar).

2. Transfer the butter to a colander. You can save the buttermilk if you would like. It's great in biscuits.

3. Squeeze the butter with your hands to get out as much of the buttermilk as possible.

4. Rinse the butter in the colander under cold water, turning and squeezing the butter until the water runs clear.

5. Transfer the butter to a bowl or onto the counter and add salt. Knead it in. Taste as you go. Add salt until your butter tastes just right.

6. Keep the butter in an airtight container for up to one month.

INDEX

AFTER-READING QUESTIONS

1. When was milk production in the United States industrialized with the use of automated milking systems?

2. When did supermarkets become common in the United States?

3. Name two reasons for sustainable farming and animal rearing.

4. What was the main reason that early cooking shows were produced and aired?

5. What do supermarkets place by the entrance, and why?

ACTIVITY

If you were going to start a show about food on social media, YouTube, or the Food Network, what would your show be about? What would it be called? Describe or film the first episode.

ABOUT THE AUTHOR

Jen Breach (pronouns: they/them) is queer and nonbinary. Jen grew up in a tiny town in rural Australia with three older brothers, two parents, and one pet duck. Jen has worked as an archaeologist, a librarian, an editor, a florist, a barista, a bagel-baker, a code-breaker, a ticket-taker, and a trouble-maker. The best job they ever had was as a writer, which they do now in Philadelphia, Pennsylvania. Jen has milked a cow with their own two hands, raised chickens for Sunday dinner, and is a big fan of TV cooking competitions.

www.rourkebooks.com

PHOTO CREDITS: Cover: Nas photo/ Shutterstock.com, Ales Krivec on Unsplash, AngieYeoh/ Shutterstock.com, Donna Beeler/ Shutterstock.com; pages 4-5: ilbusca/ Getty Images; page 6: Grafissimo/ Getty Images; page 7: Official/ Shutterstock.com; page 9: Everett Collection/ Shutterstock.com; page 9: Everett Collection/ Shutterstock.com; page 10: George Marks/ Getty Images; pages 10-11: Kwangmoozaa/ Shutterstock.com; page 11: 5m3photos/ Shutterstock.com; page 12: ilbusca/ Getty Images; pages 12-13: Aleksandr Rybalko/ Shutterstock.com; page: 14 Chat Karen Studio; page 15: Juergen Faelchle/ Shutterstock.com; page 15: Singha Songsak P/ Shutterstock.com; page 16: Pixel-Shot/ Shutterstock.com; pages 16-17: Tricky_Shark/ Shutterstock.com; page 18: New Africa/ Shutterstock.com; pages 18-19: Sunshine Seeds/ Shutterstock.com; page 20: Krasula/ Shutterstock.com; page 21: Clive Stapleton/ Shutterstock.com; page 22: EWING GALLOWAY/CLASSICSTOCK/Everett Collection; page 23: CSA Images/ Getty Images; page 23: Ronald Reagan Presidential Library; page 25: CSU Archives / Everett Collection; page 25: © Food Network / Courtesy: Everett Collection; page 27: svetikd/ Getty Images; page 27: fizkes/ Shutterstock.com; page 29: fizkes/ Shutterstock.com; page 29: andrewrakov/ Shutterstock.com; page 29: Wichy/ Shutterstock.com; page 30: Africa Studio/ Shutterstock.com; pages 1, 3, 4, 6-7, 8, 10, 12-13, 14, 16, 18, 20-22, 24, 26, 28, 30-32: Nas photo/ Shutterstock.com; pages 4, 7, 10-11, 13, 14, 20, 25, 30-32: Lana Veshta/ Shutterstock.com; pages 6-9, 14-15, 22-27, 29: Ales Krivec on Unsplash

Edited by: Catherine Malaski
Cover and interior design by: Max Porter

Library of Congress PCN Data

The Evolution of Food / Jen Breach
(Food Tour)
ISBN 978-1-73165-291-1 (hard cover)(alk. paper)
ISBN 978-1-73165-261-4 (soft cover)
ISBN 978-1-73165-321-5 (e-book)
ISBN 978-1-73165-351-2 (e-pub)
Library of Congress Control Number: 2021952177

Rourke Educational Media
Printed in the United States of America
01-2412211937